How a Book Is Made

written and illustrated by
Aliki

Thomas Y. Crowell | New York

to Margaret Clark

The various steps in the making of a book can differ from one publishing house to another;
this book shows how *this* book was made.
For their valuable and generous help, I am grateful to all
whose jobs are mentioned in the book, especially John Vitale,
Carolyn Otto, Lynnet Wilson, Sue Curnow, and Zig Ruskin.
Thanks most of all to Ginny Koeth, Al Cetta,
and

Barbara Fenton
Editor *extraordinaire*

Text composed in Century Expanded, Futura, News Gothic,
and Modern No. 20, by Linoprint Composition Co., Inc.
Color separation by Offset Separations Corp.
Printed by General Offset Company, Inc.
Jacket printed by New England Book Components, Inc.
Bound by A. Horowitz & Sons
Designed by Al Cetta
Production by Miranda Book

How a Book Is Made

Library of Congress Cataloging-in-Publication Data
Aliki.
    How a book is made.

    Summary: Describes the stages in making a book,
starting with the writing of the manuscript and the
drawing of the pictures, and explaining all the
technical processes leading to printed and bound copies.
    1. Books—Juvenile literature. 2. Book industries
and trade—Juvenile literature. 3. Publishers and
publishing—Juvenile literature. 4. Printing—Juvenile
literature. [1. Books. 2. Book industries and trade.
3. Publishers and publishing. 4. Printing] I. Title.
Z116.A2A42 1986   686   85-48156
ISBN 0-690-04496-8
ISBN 0-690-04498-4 (lib. bdg.)

I like books.

I like the way a book feels.

I like the way a book smells.

I like to turn each page,

read each word,

look at the pictures.

Who made this book?

It was Spring.

Author-Artist (Illustrator)

Editor

Publisher

Designer

Copyeditor-Proofreader

Production Director

Color Separator

Printer

Publicity and Promotion Director

Salesperson

"I did," says the author-artist.

"We did," say the editor, the publisher,

the printer, and many others.

They all did.

Many people made this book.

And this is how they did it.

A book starts with an idea.

The AUTHOR thinks of a story.

She writes it down.

It is harder than she expected.

Sometimes she can't find the right words.

She has to look things up.

A few weeks later...

Whew! I'm getting there!

Typing is neater.

FEBRUARY

DONE!

At last she is satisfied.

Good-bye, baby.

Will she like it?

She sends off her MANUSCRIPT

Editorial Department

Morning mail.

Thank you.

Another manuscript to read!

This pile gets bigger and bigger.

GOODBOOKS PUBLISHING COMPANY

to her EDITOR at Goodbooks Publishing Company.

The editor likes the story. The PUBLISHER likes it, too.

The editor sends the author a CONTRACT.

A contract is a promise. The publishing company will manufacture, publish, and sell the book, and pay the author a ROYALTY. That means the author gets some money for each copy of the book sold. The more copies that are sold, the more the author earns.

The ARTIST also gets a contract.

In this case the author is the artist.

She will illustrate her own book, so there is only one contract.

The author-artist signs the contract.

The author's work is done for now.

And now the artist's work begins.

She chooses the size and plans out the pages.

Then she makes a handmade book called a DUMMY.

She designs the dummy the way she wants the book to look.

The artist shows the dummy to her editor.

The editor makes some changes in the TEXT.

The DESIGNER makes some suggestions for the art.

They choose a TYPEFACE for the text.

The COPYEDITOR checks the spelling, grammar, and punctuation.

The designer sends the edited text to the typesetter, where it will be SET into TYPE on GALLEYS.

The text is typed into a computer where it is stored in code on a magnetic tape or floppy disk.

floppy disk

typestyle disk with all the letters of the alphabet in one typeface

The floppy disk is put into a TYPESETTING MACHINE, together with a typestyle disk. Letter by letter, the coded text is transferred from the floppy disk and set on PHOTOSENSITIVE PAPER in the chosen typeface.

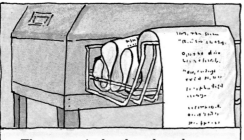

The paper is developed, and comes out with the text printed on it in one long galley, which is then cut.

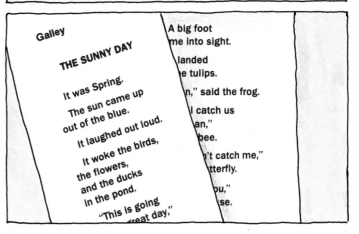

Galley

THE SUNNY DAY

It was Spring.
The sun came up
out of the blue.
It laughed out loud.
It woke the birds,
the flowers,
and the ducks
in the pond.
"This is going
    great day,"

A big foot
me into sight.

landed
e tulips.

n," said the frog.

I catch us
an,"
bee.

't catch me,"
tterfly.

u,"
se.

The PROOFREADER checks the galleys.

Another set is sent to the author-artist.

13

Now the artist has more to do.

She prepares the FINISHED ARTWORK.

She uses the dummy as a guide.

Each page is drawn separately and measured exactly.

one spread (two pages)

gutter (where the book will be sewn)

trim lines (where the pages will be cut)

Page 4   Page 5

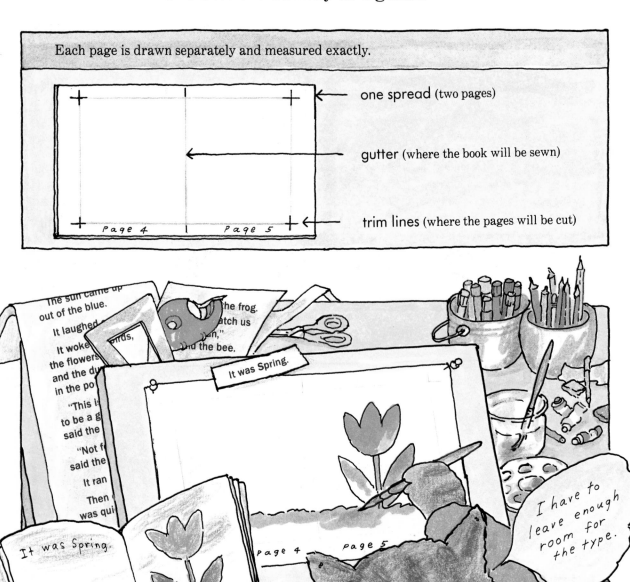

14

The art is in FULL COLOR.

It looks the way it will in the printed book.

It is a long, hard job.

The finished art is delivered.

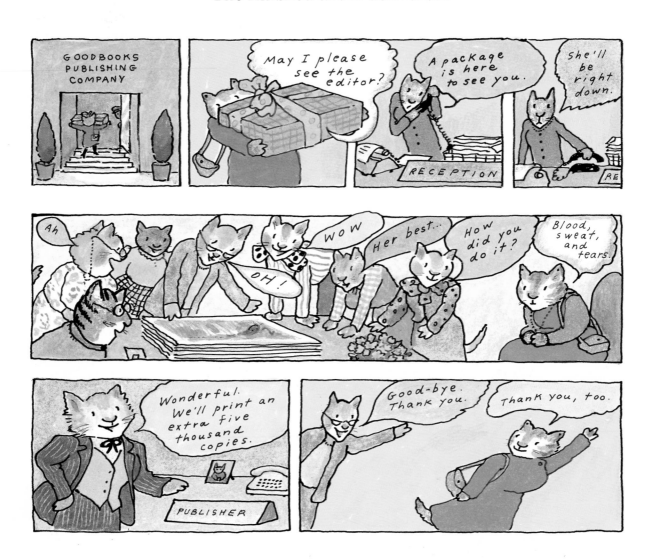

The artist's job is done.

The art is checked for any mistakes.

Then the PRODUCTION DIRECTOR makes COST ESTIMATES and
a PRODUCTION SCHEDULE and orders PAPER for the books.

The designer makes MECHANICALS.

They show exactly how the text and art will fit together.

He pastes the
galley type
onto OVERLAYS.

The art and mechanicals are sent to the COLOR SEPARATOR where FILMS will be made.

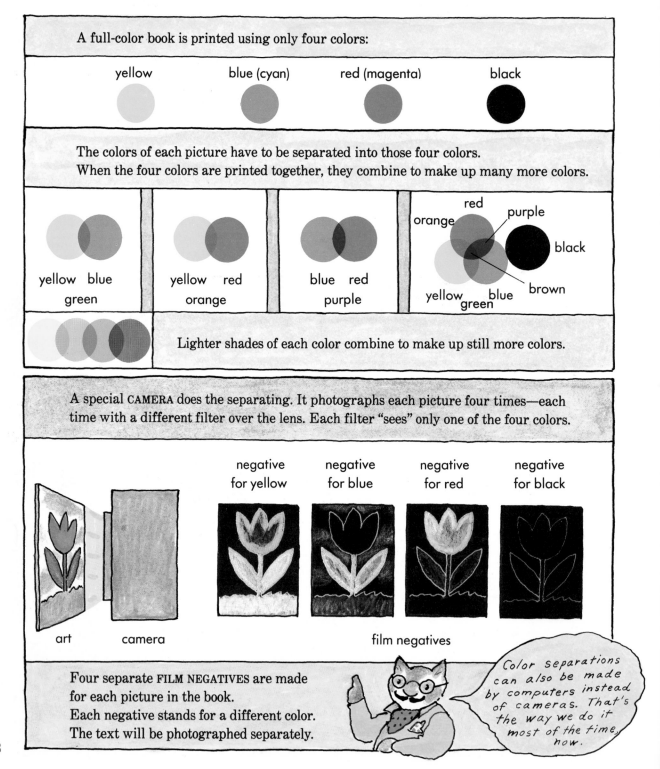

A full-color book is printed using only four colors:

yellow   blue (cyan)   red (magenta)   black

The colors of each picture have to be separated into those four colors.
When the four colors are printed together, they combine to make up many more colors.

yellow   blue
green

yellow   red
orange

blue   red
purple

red   purple
orange   black
                        brown
yellow   blue
      green

Lighter shades of each color combine to make up still more colors.

A special CAMERA does the separating. It photographs each picture four times—each time with a different filter over the lens. Each filter "sees" only one of the four colors.

negative
for yellow

negative
for blue

negative
for red

negative
for black

art   camera   film negatives

Four separate FILM NEGATIVES are made
for each picture in the book.
Each negative stands for a different color.
The text will be photographed separately.

Color separations can also be made by computers instead of cameras. That's the way we do it most of the time, now.

Sometimes the art is PRESEPARATED by the artist. A separate overlay is made for each color. The overlays will be photographed to make the film negatives.

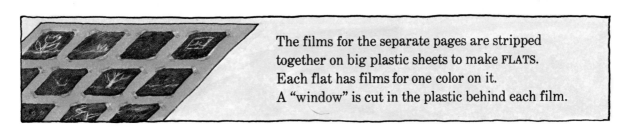

overlay

register marks to keep the separate overlays correctly lined up with one another

Page 4   Red   Page 5
Page 4   Blue   Page 5
Page 4   Yellow   Page 5

Black   Page 5

100%
70%
50%
30%
10%

s Spring.

The art is painted in shades of black. The shades of black stand for shades of the four different printing colors. The artist has to know all the color combinations and how to show them in shades of black.

The films are put together by the STRIPPER.

The films for the separate pages are stripped together on big plastic sheets to make FLATS.
Each flat has films for one color on it.
A "window" is cut in the plastic behind each film.

Then PRINTING PLATES are made from the films.

There are separate plates for each color.

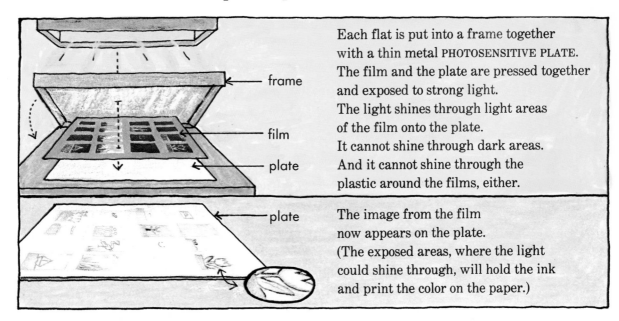

frame

film

plate

plate

Each flat is put into a frame together with a thin metal PHOTOSENSITIVE PLATE.
The film and the plate are pressed together and exposed to strong light.
The light shines through light areas of the film onto the plate.
It cannot shine through dark areas.
And it cannot shine through the plastic around the films, either.

The image from the film now appears on the plate.
(The exposed areas, where the light could shine through, will hold the ink and print the color on the paper.)

The plates are used to make COLOR PROOFS.
The proofs will be checked to see if the printed colors
match the artwork.

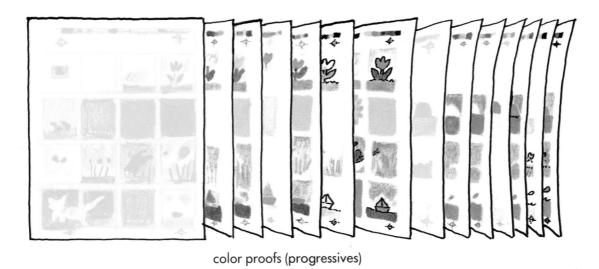

color proofs (progressives)

The four colors are printed separately, then in combinations,
and then all together.

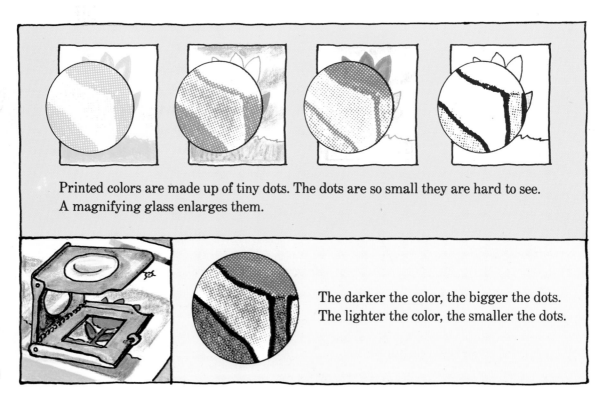

Printed colors are made up of tiny dots. The dots are so small they are hard to see.
A magnifying glass enlarges them.

The darker the color, the bigger the dots.
The lighter the color, the smaller the dots.

20

The color separator looks to see if the colors are too strong or too light. Through the magnifying glass, he can see if the colors are properly REGISTERED— that the dots are printed in the right positions.

Everyone checks the proofs very carefully.

Corrections are made on the films and new plates are made.

A final proof is printed and approved.

The blue is too strong overall.

The red doesn't match the art. Let's add some yellow.

I think it's out of register here.

The "progs" help us see which colors may need correction.

The films of the art and text are put together and exposed to light to make a BLUEPRINT.

This is the last chance to check and correct the films.

Now the set of FINAL PRINTING PLATES can be made.

All thirty-two PAGES are arranged so that they will print on one big SHEET.

Some pages are upside down.

After the printing, the sheets will be folded again and again.

Each page will fall into the right place.

Sixteen pages are on one side of the sheet…

1	16	13	4
8	9	12	5
17	32	29	20
24	25	28	21

sixteen pages are on the other.

3	14	15	2
6	11	10	7
19	30	31	18
22	27	26	23

The COVER and JACKET will be printed separately.

F I N A L L Y...

The plates are put on the big cylinders
of a FOUR-COLOR PRINTING PRESS.

The book goes "on press."

After months of preparation, the printing takes only a day.

The noisy four-color press is in a huge room with other presses.

Inside the Four-Color Offset Printing Press

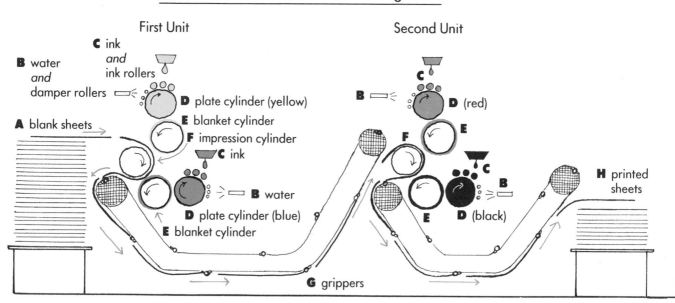

First Unit

C ink *and* ink rollers

B water *and* damper rollers

A blank sheets

D plate cylinder (yellow)
E blanket cylinder
F impression cylinder
C ink
B water
D plate cylinder (blue)
E blanket cylinder

Second Unit

C
B
D (red)
E
F
C
B
E
D (black)

H printed sheets

G grippers

Enough sheets are printed to make all the copies of the book—
first one side of the sheet, then the other.

The first sheets are checked. When the color is perfect, the rest of the sheets are printed.
When one job is finished, the machines are cleaned for the next job.

Each unit of the press prints two colors at a time.
The inks and the machinery are controlled from the CONTROL PANEL.

1. Blank sheets **A** are stacked at one end of the press.
2. The plates on the plate cylinders **D** are dampened with water **B** and inked **C**.
3. The image from each plate is printed onto the rubber blanket cylinders **E**.
4. As the sheet passes between the first blanket cylinder **E** and the metal impression cylinder **F**,
   and then between the impression cylinder and the second blanket cylinder **E**,
   the ink impressions from the blanket cylinders are printed onto the sheet.
5. Grippers **G** pull the partially printed sheet to the next printing unit.
6. After four color impressions, the printed sheets **H** are pulled by another set of grippers
   and stacked at the other end of the press.

The press can print thousands of sheets an hour.

The PRINTED SHEETS are sent to the BINDERY.

Sheets are cut in half and then folded…

into two SIGNATURES—sixteen pages each.

They are FOLDED,   GATHERED,

The signatures are still folded at the edges.

The edges are trimmed off.

SEWN,   and TRIMMED.

One sheet has become thirty-two pages.

A hard COVER is made.

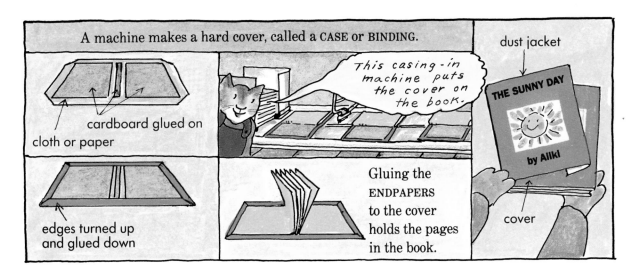

A machine makes a hard cover, called a CASE or BINDING.

cardboard glued on cloth or paper

edges turned up and glued down

This casing-in machine puts the cover on the book.

Gluing the ENDPAPERS to the cover holds the pages in the book.

dust jacket

THE SUNNY DAY
by Aliki

cover

A DUST JACKET is wrapped around the book.

dust jacket

spine

signatures

cover

front flap

back flap

endpapers

A bound copy! It looks great!

This was worth waiting for!

Let's celebrate!

At last—a BOUND BOOK!

The bound books are taken to the warehouse and stored.

The editor presents the book at SALES CONFERENCE.

Copies of the book are sent to newspapers and magazines and to librarians.

The book is talked about and REVIEWED.

Librarians buy copies for their libraries.

The SALESPEOPLE sell the book to bookstores.

One day Father sees the book. He buys it.

A book for me!

I can read it.

I can smell it.

I can keep it forever.

Then they began to howl, first her father, then her mother, then all the rest. And this time Hanni joined in. She lifted her head and howled magnificently. From deep inside, her song came pouring out. At last Hanni was adding her voice to the song of her family.

To Katie and Lily, my youngest nieces
—W.H.

For Will and Jean
—J.K.

Oil paints were used for the full-color illustrations. The text type is 14-point Dutch 811.

Text copyright © 1998 by Will Hobbs. Illustrations copyright © 1998 by Jill Kastner.

Published by Morrow Junior Books, a division of William Morrow and Company, Inc., 1350 Avenue of the Americas, New York, NY 10019

Manufactured in China by South China Printing Co. Ltd.

10 9 8 7

Library of Congress Cataloging-in-Publication Data
Hobbs, Will.
Howling Hill/by Will Hobbs; illustrated by Jill Kastner.
p. cm.
Summary: While separated from her family in the wilderness area along the Nahanni River,
a wolf pup discovers that she can express her loneliness in a long, loud howl.
ISBN 0-688-15429-8 (trade)—ISBN 0-688-15430-1 (library)
[1. Wolves—Fiction.   2. Wilderness areas—Fiction.]   I. Kastner, Jill, ill.   II. Title.   PZ7.H6524Ho 1998   [E]—dc21   97-32915   GIP AC